About The Author

Jim Kincaid, born in Texas, grew up in rural Arkansas and had to work for a living very early on. A printer's devil, a typesetter, a soda jerk, theater usher, short order cook, and general laborer. Finally, he learned the communications business and grew up with the industry.

When sent out as a young reporter by the city editor at WCBS in New York to cover the story about an illegal whiskey still in the Bronx, Jim came back with a "quality control" check and noted how the pipes were not of copper as they should be. You might say, he missed the point. Or, did he? Kincaid sees which way the crowd is running, and walks in the opposite direction. He gets the personal story.

During the Vietnam war he reported for ABC News from the field wherever the real action was. Badly wounded in a helicopter crash, he recovered in Hong Kong and returned to the U.S. in 1971 to the ABC Chicago Bureau. He left ABC for a quieter life in Virginia where he has been anchoring the local news in Hampton Roads since 1978. He has written three books and recently completed a documen ed a documen   irrently in the   on
World War I   its
movement ir   ne
between his   his
farm in rural

To ─ Ivonne & Cody
Thanks with love
Jim Kincaid
2-21-96

Théo

Theodore Wildanger

1905-1989

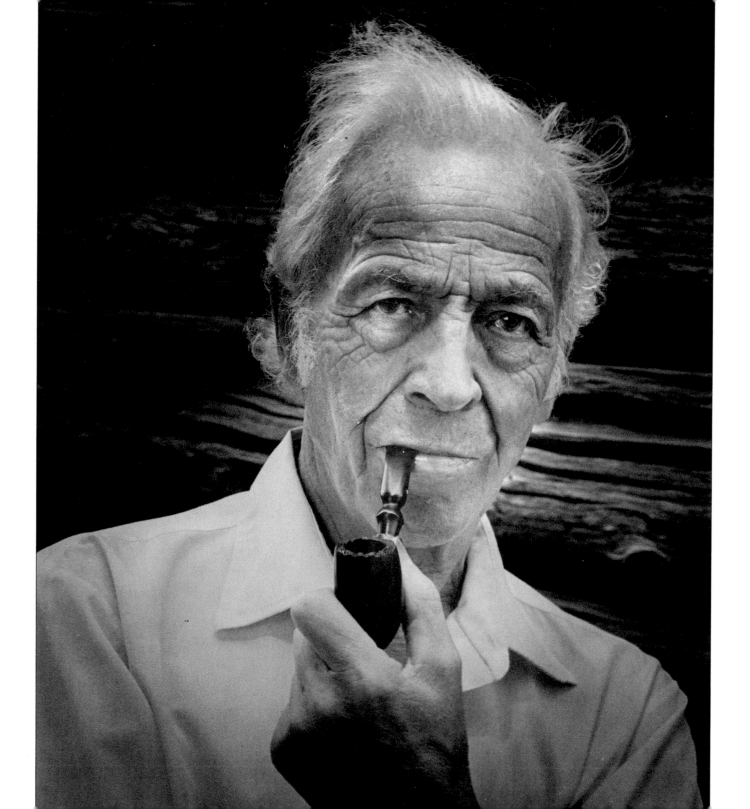

ISBN 0-9643111-0-0
ISBN 0-9643111-1-9

For more information on any of these works, or for a complete listing of original paintings and sculptures, please contact:

Wildanger Collection, Ltd. P.O. Box 175, Norfolk, VA 23501

Théo

By
Jim Kincaid

To Anna

"Les Bords De La Seine"   oil on canvas   24" x 30"
Courtesy Swayne Family

Foreword
Ann Dearsley-Vernon

Introduction
Marge Swayne

"Elam Dream Scene"   oil on stretched canvas   24" x 30"   Private Collection

Book Design
Sarah Mathis-Weeks

Photography
Glen McClure

Portrait
Frank Jones

Acknowledgments

The "birthing" of a book such as this requires more "parents" than the conventional baby, and I must share the pride of authorship with some very special people.

David Delpierre combined his legal expertise and eye for art in so many ways for the establishment of the Wildanger Collection Ltd and this book. Sarah Weeks, an artist in her own right, labored skillfully for many hours on the design and layout. We are indebted to Barbara Mason for the distinctive "Theo" logo, to Glen McClure for the excellent photography, and to Frank Jones, who took the portrait of Theo while on a visit to Elam some years ago.

I can't say enough about my fellow writers...Marge Swayne, who knew Theo well, as a neighbor; and Ann Dearsley-Vernon, who "met" him at the working level through his paintings; "Nina Dear", whose ongoing affair with Theo's art borders on obsession...

And finally, to Catherine, who believed this book "should" be done, and saw to it that it "could" be done.

Foreword

In 1989 I met Theo Wildanger for the first time. He was presented to me by his daughter Catherine Kincaid at a lively party that Theo would have surely enjoyed. The past tense is appropriate, because the handsome, quintessentially European artist had died earlier the same year. And so, instead of shaking hands and listening to Theo's Luxembourg-Parisian greeting, my initial introduction was through a small selection of flower paintings rather than through the painter himself. From the beginning, Theo's exuberant spirit was obvious in every blossom, in every brush stroke, every gesture; this is how our friendship began.

The small, dense, opaque, jewel-like flowers that comprised my first glimpse into Theo Wildanger's private world were only a tantalizing hint of the huge collection of paintings and objects that he created before his death at age 84. Wanting to know more about both the artist and his work, I requested an invitation to Catherine and Jim Kincaid's elegant turn of the century Norfolk home where Theo's work was temporarily stored in the basement. Basements in Norfolk are relatively rare because of the high water table; to observe that the Kincaids owned one of the driest, cleanest basements in town was certainly a relief!

The extent of this previously unseen collection was a startling surprise. Here were hundreds upon hundreds of paintings on every kind of surface from paper to tin, displaying a correspondingly wide array of subject matter. Trusting my suggestions, Catherine and her daughter Caroline quickly and efficiently assumed the roles of curator and registrar. Each of Theo's flat

"The Flower Garden"
oil on stretched canvas
24" x 30"
Courtesy Wall Family

works was separated with acid free paper. Canvases were properly placed in racks designed to permit air circulation. Caroline assigned a number to every object, recording the title, dimensions, and condition. Framing began. Marketing was initiated. A lengthy, illustrated newspaper article appeared in 'The Virginian Pilot/Ledger Star', as Theo was introduced to an increasing number of friends and admirers.

The Hampton Roads community became increasingly aware of the work of Theo Wildanger in 1993 through two major exhibitions and the Kincaids' generous donation of his work to an AIDS benefit auction. Additionally, Nina Newby-Ireland became an informal agent for the paintings, placing work in various east coast locations, Canada, and Paris. How pleased Theo would have been to know that his creative efforts had come full circle in the City of Lights!

Jim Kincaid's loving tribute to his father-in-law of almost two decades is presented in the following pages. The words and the images together provide a vibrant echo of an immensely talented, complicated artist. Theo Wildanger's visual vocabulary ranges from sensual nudes to tormented figures of Christ crucified; from shipwreck victims in a raging sea to serene Elam landscapes; from monochromatic, desperate figures to an abundance of brilliantly petaled bouquets. Whatever the subject, Theo's work is intensely personal, and always comes from the heart.

The artist that I never knew is present and available through his art in this book. It is a pleasure to introduce him!

Ann Dearsley-Vernon,
Director of Education
The Chrysler Museum

"Maria Callas"
oil on canvas
24" x 30"

Introduction

To know art as a general rule is to know the artist: in Theo Wildanger's case to know his art is to know Elam. The bold strokes, the vibrant colors, the lines and contrast all speak of the rural community that he loved. Elam was, in fact, the only common ground that Theo and I shared. He was a senior-aged man of European lineage; I was a middle-aged woman of midwestern background. As an artist he focused on the emotional; as a journalist I was trained to filter out emotions and concentrate on the facts.

We didn't speak the same language, and although he was too polite to say so, he often didn't understand my way of doing things. We both, however, shared a love for Elam and a dog named Fifi, and that as it turned out was enough to form a friendship.

It was Fifi, in fact, who made the formal introductions. "Hello, madame," a voice not entirely comfortable with either the telephone or the English language would say: "This is Theo, is Fifi there?" When I replied in the affirmative I could sense the relief in Theo's voice. "Tell her - come home please."

"Wash Day"
oil on particle board
17" x 20"

When I relayed this message to Fifi she would rouse herself from a comfortable sleeping position on the deck, wave her plumed tail in a jaunty good-by, and trot off for home without a backward glance. There was a special closeness between Fifi and Theo that went beyond dog and master. While Theo worked on his paintings the English Setter dozed in a chair nearby. When the artist took his daily constitutional, Fifi followed close behind. Neighbors maintained that they could set their clocks by the sight of Theo and Fifi ambling down the road to inspect a possible subject for a painting.

When spring arrived Theo and Fifi took to the road in earnest. With sturdy walking stick in hand the artist sometimes hiked a mile or more to study the sun-dappled shading of irises and peonies growing on a neighbor's farm. Spring speaks to all of us in one way or another. Spring not only spoke to Theo, she whispered secrets that no one else seemed to hear. Once when I complained of a rainy day, the artist knitted his bushy eyebrows in concern and mildly admonished me. "The rain is good, madame," he said. "It makes spring the beauty time!"

Theo's paintings often expressed that beauty time by touching on religion - in small ways such as a steeple and cross tucked into a landscape, or in truly grandiose fashion with his depiction of the crucifixion. His neighbors at Elam sensed that the artist walked close to God. He never missed a Sunday at Olive Branch Methodist Church.

"In fact, I am not a Methodist; I belong to the Catholic church," he once told me. "But is okay," he added pointing his ever present pipe toward the heavens. "We all pray to the same God."

The Rev. Tom Walthal, pastor of the church, was concerned that Theo might not understand his Southern inflection. "Do you understand my sermons?' he once asked Theo. "No," he replied shaking his head with a typically gracious smile. "But I like to hear the words."

Theo not only heard the words, he lived them. His concern for his neighbors was sincere. When my granddaughter was hospitalized Theo heard that she was very ill and became concerned. Because he did not drive and had no way of getting to the hospital the artist gave the only comfort he was able to offer. The painting he presented to the recovering child was in soothing shades of green. An artist critic who later viewed the painting explained that green was the color of healing. What Theo could not give on a personal level, he gave of a greater gift - the gift of his spirit.

He gave paintings to wood cutters, to visitors who admired them, to friends and to neighbors. During one particularly bad winter when the roads were impassable to vehicles, I walked over to see if Theo was all right. He insisted on giving me one of his largest paintings, and so I slipped and slid all the way home carefully holding the work of art. When the former pastor of Olive Branch Church was scheduled to leave for another church, Theo went to work on a farewell gift - a painting of the Last Supper. The congregation had it framed and it was presented to the departing minister. The list could go on and on.

Theo loved his friends at Elam and they loved him back. It was the congregation of Olive Branch Church that first sensed something amiss when Theo did not appear at church one Sunday morning. He was, in fact, ill and shortly after that Theo left Elam for good to live at a local retirement home. We all grieved in some way to see him go; Fifi took it especially to heart. The next day she was trotting down the road when a car hit her. Fifi was buried in a grove of pines behind Theo's studio that afternoon.

A year later Theo came home as well. His ashes were scattered in the same peaceful glen where Fifi was buried. Half a decade has passed since Theo's death. Elam has changed in subtle ways, but the art of Theo Wildanger has not.

opposite page
"Storm at Elam"
oil on canvas board
24" x 36"

X

When I look at Theo's paintings, I see the bright colors, the bold lines, and his masterful way with light and contrast; but I see something else as well. I see Theo and Fifi forever surrounded by spring flowers. As any one of the members of Olive Branch Church will tell you, that is exactly where he is at this moment.

I speak for the entire community of Elam when I say that we were blessed to have him in our midst. Theo showed us the "beauty time" in so many ways, and not only with his art. He would, I know, be immeasurably pleased to see that beauty being shared with the world.

Marge Swayne, Lifestyles Editor
The Farmville Herald

opposite page
"Aumetz" 1969
oil on paper
8.5" x 11"

Walking into the ancient streets of Aumetz, a tiny and not very important town in northeastern France, was almost like traveling in time.

It was not the village of 1992, but a town embedded in my memory in countless conversations with Theo, a town of more than three quarters of a century ago, and there, there, a few hundred yards from the village square, was the farmhouse.

It was, perhaps, not the very house where Theo had been farmed out, by his father, to watch the farmer's cows, but it fit the description exactly.

Let me take you back to that time, early in this century, when the world was as troubled as it is today. Borders were in dispute. Politicians were calling the shots. And the people were trying to live with the uncertainty that always follows when politicians call the shots.

Aumetz is located in the northeastern part of France now. But in those days it was believed, indeed it was possible, that Aumetz was really a part of Germany. Nobody seemed to know for sure, but all who had an opinion were certain that theirs was the only opinion that really counted.

"The Farmhouse in Aumetz"
oil on paper, 1969
8.5" x 11"
Private Collection

Is it any wonder then, that a boy born into a large family that tried to avoid politics, should grow up with very little sense of belonging to one nation or another? After all, the Alsatian region had been bartered, fought for, traded, and negotiated back and forth between Germans and the French for generations.

Catherine, Theo's daughter, and I had decided in the summer of 1991 that we should go to the land of Theo's birth, to his beginnings, to study, confirm perhaps, to try to solidify the things we knew, or thought we knew, about what made him the man he was.

So, we found ourselves the following summer trying to retrace some of his steps. Our only roadmap, the stories he told around the dinner table at Elam, our retreat in Prince Edward County, Virginia.

Theo was quite a storyteller. And for one who fancies himself a storyteller, that is the highest form of praise.

It was some years into my relationship with Theo that I realized what a great storyteller he was and that he had a medium, his paints, that carried him far beyond his spoken languages. And I use the plural here, because Theo spoke several languages with great fluency. My great regret was that English was not among them. But, by and by, his smattering of English, and my smattering of German, and trace of French, and our common respect for Latin, enabled us to develop a language which we two spoke fluently, to the exclusion of the remainder of humanity.

When Theo would cry out from his painting station on the back porch of the old farmhouse at Elam, "Zhim...komm...I haf mak a beauty ting", I would know I was about to be introduced to a new painting. And, a "beauty thing" it would surely be. Sometimes a dark beauty. Sometimes sharp and accusing. But always a "beauty thing".

And, he turned out these "beauty things" with such grace, it was hard to appreciate the ease with which he spoke his most fluent language. All that was dear to him would appear on the canvas by and by. And he hardly ever felt the need to explain what he meant by this or that, it was simply a novel he was writing, and it was up to the reader to determine what he meant.

Over the course of years, I was finally able to decipher some of what he was saying, and, I hope eyes more educated and skillful than mine will continue to probe his thoughts. But, in the end, he created a "beauty thing" of vast scope, a body of work that depicted life as he saw it, through the eyes of a man without a country, but who was at home in all countries, because he shared the hopes and pains and gladnesses and sorrows of his kinsmen, the human race.

As Catherine and I walked through the streets of Aumetz, I was able to see with my own eyes the little boy he had described to me. The child whose family had to scramble for their daily meal. The child who tended a farmer's

ink on paper
8.5" x 11"
Private Collection

cows in hopes of a piece of bread for supper, thus relieving his father of the burden of feeding him from very meager resources, the child who labored in the local mines, when he was old enough to push a tram; and, when an accident claimed a part of his hand, was not consulted when the mining company paid his father a few pennies for the missing finger. That Theo would become an artist, a great artist, was not in the cards dealt to him in the village of Aumetz.

Future examiners of his work would see the blackness of the mines, and the terror, in the lines which accentuate some of his darker works. Indeed, he found the civil rights struggle in America to be not unlike his own struggle for survival. You will see it in his "Street Scene", (opposite page) and perhaps even in his flowers from time to time.

Foy Casper, the eminent art historian and restorer, once described Theo's flowers, the overwhelming majority of his works, as simply "scales". The scales a musician does while waiting for the real music to come. Practice, to keep the eye and hand in tune for the "major" performance ahead.

Street Scene
oil on tin
28" x 33"

I don't know. Perhaps it is so, but I always felt that Theo painted flowers because they gave him peace. Much like I write something light, or funny, between my serious pieces to comfort myself, and throw the audience off my track, so they'll be there, unsuspecting, when I have something serious to tell them.

And Theo had serious things to tell them.

In his "Judgment" (opposite page) the plight of the common man facing the assembled power of the state, the church, the bureaucracy, is devastatingly reflected in the stooped shoulder and helplessness of the figure in the foreground. You'll note that his judges have more faces than ordinary humans are equipped with; but, in Theo's world, judges needed them. In his growing up, Theo had faced these assembled powers himself, and found that, when justice and politics collided, politics generally won; and that the judges, for survival's sake, often used one set of eyes to see the justice of a matter, and another to see the political necessity. In the "Judgment", he tells the story of a people, and a time, when this was not simply true, but the accepted order of things.

It pleases me beyond measure to be able to tell you that he modified these opinions late in life, after living in America for nearly twenty years, and had finally decided to become a man "with" a country. In the last year of his life,

"Judgment"
oil on streched canvas
24" x 30"

perhaps his most prolific as a painter, he was studying hard to learn the things he had to know to become a citizen of the United States. I was, in fact, his coach in the matter of the "Pledge of Allegiance", and can faithfully report that his favorite phrase of all was "With Liberty And Justice For All." I think, if he had lived to deliver the pledge, and that line, before a federal judge, that the judge would have granted immediate citizenship, and Theo would have changed his opinion of judges.

His opinions about politics, or, more to the point, politicians, were destined to remain firmly in place.

But, he realized, and appreciated the fact, that of all places on earth, America was the one, at least the only one he knew, where he could pick up his brushes and say anything on the canvas that he wanted to say, and that no one could do anything about it. And, that was what painting was for Theo. The opportunity to say what he wanted to say, and to care little about what anyone thought about it.

"Post Card"
oil on illustration board
4" x 6"

One of his greatest pleasures lay in the fact that he never sold a painting. Thus, he had broken Van Gogh's record. Van Gogh sold one, probably for rent money, and Theo often told his admirers so; and then, reaching into a disorderly stack he would select a piece, and say "dis is for you. I gif it you, tak care, in ze time, it mak you rich!" Thus, the body of Theo's work is represented in collections far and wide. The collections of serious patrons of the arts, and the bedroom walls of plumbers, chimney cleaners, and bailers of hay. Hardly anyone ever came to Elam and stayed for more than a few hours, without being shown to his studio and through his stacks of paintings and, finally, leaving with a painting under his or her arm. Theo had no doubt, not the slightest, that his paintings had great value; but he wanted to remain untouched by any sort of thought that he would do such things for money. He had known painters who painted for money, and he knew that most of them, if not all of them, painted with an eye to what somebody might want to buy. He was deeply afraid that even one sale might tempt him to do likewise.

"Elvis"
oil on canvas
28" x 33"

When I discussed this with him, he would dismiss the idea. "Dat is for Doris" (his daughter, Theodora Catherine, my wife) "und de Peepchen" (his grand-daughter, Carolyn) "ven I am no more here."

On one occasion, before we moved to Elam, I persuaded him to offer one of his paintings for a charity auction for Carolyn's school. He agreed, but on the condition that I require a minimum bid far beyond the pocketbooks of the auction's attendees. I gradually became aware that he simply didn't want to sell a part of his life cheaply, to see something that was dear to him profaned with an insulting offer. He preferred to "gif it you", knowing that a great value would someday be realized.

Some years later, after we came to Hampton Roads, and after Theo's death, Catherine and I were persuaded to offer one of his pieces for an auction to benefit Candii House, a wonderful institution in Norfolk involving people of many faiths in the care and happiness, for a few short years, of children born with AIDS.

We selected a delightful little piece, beautifully framed, and when it came up for bid, I was privileged to announce the sale. Remembering Theo's formula (we really didn't want to part with it), I told the audience that there would be a minimum bid, and if it was not sold for at least that amount, we would retain it, and, at such time as it might sell, give the proceeds to Candii House. It brought much more than the amount I requested; and watching it depart with a very worthy owner, I felt something like you feel when you've sold something dear, or given away a cat. You know the new owner will appreciate it and care for it and treasure it, but, oh, how you'll miss it.

In fact, Catherine and I were to have that feeling numerous times in the coming few years.

We had decided to take on the project that Theo had assigned to us during the last few years of his life. That being, to get his paintings in front of as many people as possible. To do whatever we could to enable him to say what he had to say to all who would take the time to listen.

"Fleurs et Vin"
oil on stretched canvas
24" x 18"

To listen with their eyes, and their hearts, and he cared little about whether the audience would be trained in art, or just people who knew what they liked, and found his stories something they could relate to their own lives or experiences.

We knew this would involve parting with some of his pieces, but we didn't know how hard that would eventually turn out to be.

On several occasions we had shown a number of paintings, with no eye whatsoever to sell, but merely to display.

"Horses"
oil on canvas
18" x 24"
Private Collection

Finally, in 1992 we mounted a serious show at Harbor Gallery in Norfolk of thirty odd paintings, among them some of the best and some of our personal favorites; and, for the first time, had to deal with the idea of putting price tags on most of them. Some, it turned out in the decision process, were and remain, beyond our capability to price.

But we had to steel ourselves to the idea that Theo's paintings would become known to the rest of the world only by being disseminated among those who would appreciate his art, and that, alas, involved "selling" them. At least, some of them. And there was the rub. Within a few minutes of that first opening, the gallery owner came to me with the news that a piece had been sold, and she was probably somewhat surprised that I did not receive the news with unbridled joy. Of course, I was complimented, and gratified that the recognition of his work came so quickly, but I was not surprised, and indeed, I was almost dreading the revelation as to what piece it was, sure in my heart that it would be one that would be hard to see go into other hands.

"Le Reve"
oil on canvas board
30" x 24"

It was a very successful show, and Catherine and I exulted at every sale, and grieved at every impending departure. I envy those who live with genius, and don't recognize it as genius, and thus don't have deep and personal attachments to each artifact.

I had never considered until I saw Theo's first paintings go to new homes, how very fortunate I was to be a writer instead. I can give away, or sell what I do, and keep a copy that is in every way as good as the original. Writing, after all, is just an arrangement of words, and once arranged, those words can be reproduced as many times as one cares to, with no diminishment in quality.

A painting, on the other hand, can be photographed, but it can never be quite the same as the original. It was very hard to part with those originals, even though we have excellent transparencies of each and every one, because they were the very canvases, or boards, or sheets of paper that had been lovingly adorned with oils by Theo's own hands.

While we are on the subject of galleries, Palmer-Rae of Norfolk mounted a show in July 1993, which was originally to be for a set period, but the owners keep it hanging until this 'writing'. It is indeed possible if you were to pay a visit to Palmer-Rae Gallery that you might see some of Theo's works even at this 'reading'. It is even possible that they may allow you to purchase one.

When I mention canvases, boards, or sheets of paper, let me step aside for a moment and point out that Theo never allowed convention to get in his way. There were periods of prosperity when we could afford to supply Theo with proper canvases and drawing paper. But, there were also lean times when spare money was hard to come by, and that didn't slow his production to any noticeable degree. Theo considered a surface without paint on it to be wasted space, and when canvases were not at hand, he adorned bottles, pieces of plywood, glass panes from old windows, scraps of roofing tin, peculiarly shaped tree limbs, rocks, little used pieces of furniture, old cross-cut saw blades, and odd chunks of fire wood. If a smooth river rock came into the house by any hand, mine, or Catherine's, or Carolyn's, it would soon be

"Anna's Eyes" 1976
oil on canvas
18" x 24"
Private Collection

graced with a flower, or a face, and if it happened to be a face, the eyes were invariably powerful, and looked back at you with the intensity you'll see in "Anna's Eyes", a portrait of his wife, the only woman he ever loved. Theo enjoyed the company of women and never failed to charm them with his "Old World" grace, but Anna was his first, and final romantic attachment.

To the hearty disapproval of both families, Theo and Anne-Marie ran away to Paris in the late 1920s, there to follow her dreams of theatre, and his of art.

It was during those years in Paris that Theo "learned the trade" working at such jobs as he could find, but landing some that kept him close to art and artists.

One such job was for a certain Count Trotti, a wealthy Parisian dealer in art and antiques; and while in his employ, Theo was exposed to an educational opportunity that few young men of his day would either appreciate, or take full advantage of. But for Theo it was as close as he would ever get to so called "higher" learning, and he knew it. He absorbed the facts and lore and cared little that, most of the time, he was living on the edge of poverty. After all, in his world, that was what artists were supposed to do. He met and formed a fast friendship with Rene Magritte, and came away from that friendship with a small painting by Magritte which remains in our family today. I learned this only much later, many years later, when he showed me a delightful little painting of "my friend Magritte" as casually as you might show me a favorite pen knife your father used to carry.

It was also many years after the time in Paris, that Theo demonstrated to me the profound depth of his studies in the City of Lights. I had arranged for him to visit a very well known historic house in Washington, D.C. I won't tell you precisely where, but suffice it to say that the ladies who run this institution are exceedingly proud of their American heritage, and in the case of the historic house, just as proud of the "American" artifacts therein.

oil on driftwood
40" mounted
Private Collection

As we were being guided from room to room by a docent, Theo noticed, from behind the ever present velvet rope barrier, a beautiful desk, and stated, with an authority that he always carried like a Mississippi State trooper's badge, that the desk was French. The docent was amused, and a jot annoyed, and assured him that it was an American piece of uncertain authorship. Theo was just as amused, but not really annoyed, and informed the lady that, if she would take the trouble to remove a certain drawer, she would find the signature of the "French" cabinet maker who had, "I am zorry madame, make dat". To satisfy this crazy, but kindly old man, she did reverently remove the drawer, and the signature was there, precisely where Theo had said it would be, and done by the hand of the man he had named. I have often wondered how the docent solved that problem. If the desk was removed for not being American enough, or the signature removed, or if the docent simply did the politic thing and let the matter drop. But, when next you visit our nation's capital, and the occasion to visit some landmark house arises, where the

Chincoteague Ponies   oil on tin   37.5" x 25.5"   Courtesy Sture Sigfred and Deborah Kuban

hostesses are generationally pure Americans, and the history of the country took place, to some extent, in that very house...just be aware in an upstairs parlor, the desk is French! It might be fun, if you see such a house, to ask your guide to remove the middle drawer on the right hand side, and look at the back of it--just for fun. Then smile somewhat sadly and knowingly, and go on your way. Some things are better left unsaid. Theo had a problem with that concept. If it needed to be said, he said it. It never occurred to him that such a habit might be found troublesome in some quarters.

Indeed, it was remarkable, when one came to think about it that Theo, living as he did during that difficult time between and among European wars, and the politics of it all, that he did not become, with his habit of saying what he thought about things, the guest of honor before a firing squad.

He never held back, in his painting, or his conversation. If something was on his mind, he got it off, and there were many times that I was glad that his grasp of the English language was not such that his listeners knew, as I did, exactly what he meant by what he was saying. He was invariably polite, but explicit.

"Le Bain"   oil/charcoal on paper   11" x 8.5"

One of the better illustrations of this is found in a story told me many times, about one of the jobs he held during his lean years in Paris.

He had been employed by the manager of a small theatre, a sort of vaudeville theatre, as the assistant to the lighting director. His job, to put it simply, was to mount a small stand in the wings of the stage, and try to keep light on the comics, or dancers, or trained dogs, or whoever and whatever was being presented for the edification of the audience. Many of them came armed with assorted groceries, with which to offer their criticism of the performance.

There came a time when the manager of the theatre brought his wife to a performance, and directed the lighting director, Theo's boss, to seat her in the wings on the lighting stand, so that she might have a privileged view of the events on stage.

The rub lay in the fact that the lady, how can I put it charitably, was the product of many years of good French cooking, and had retained something of each of those calorie laden meals, and was rather wider than the railings of the ladder that led to the platform in question.

So, the lighting director and Theo had to help her ascend. A process which required both of them to get behind her and push this person of great caloric consequence, up the steps.

They did so, it seems, with rather more force than was warranted, since when the lady cleared the confines of the railing at the top of the steps, the pressure holding her back was relieved, and they launched her, not onto the platform as they had designed, but rather beyond it....onto the stage, where a hapless comic team was in the process of boring the audience to the point of violence. The audience, thinking the sudden appearance of this monument to French

cuisine was part of the act, responded warmly. She brought down the house.

But the manager, the husband of the entertainment, was not amused. He, as is so often the case when blame has to be assessed along a chain of command, found Theo at the bottom, tried and convicted him in seconds, and fired him on the spot. Theo, with his usual diplomacy, said to the manager, "Sir, you should instead give me a raise, this is the first time one of your audiences has had anything to laugh about in months."

The dismissal stood.

"Pause"
oil on canvas
24" x 18"

48

Ch.Wildanger.

PAUSE

Another time, when Theo was in the employ of Count Trotti, he was dispatched, along with another employee, to the count's residence where he kept a store of fine wines.

Theo always considered himself a good judge of fine wines; and since those wines Count Trotti had instructed him to pick up, and load into a cart, were for a grand party soon to be held at the gallery, Theo felt it incumbent on him, as a faithful employee, to be sure that the selection was up to the standards he knew Count Trotti would expect. This of course required him, on gaining entrance to the count's cellar, to sample the wines. And to sample them thoroughly enough to be sure. And to require his fellow employee, and trusted friend, to do the same. After researching the wines extensively, Theo and his partner loaded several dozens of bottles into a cart Count Trotti had provided, and proceeded to trundle it back to the noble count's place of business.

En route, they chanced to pass a hotel. A grand hotel, where a person of consequence had just arrived in his Hispano-Suiza, one of the world's most expensive motorcars in that day, and when Theo and his cohort came by they managed to rake the cart down one side of this exquisite piece of machinery. Of course, the authorities were called for, and a "flic" who happened to be nearby, showed up promptly. One of the great French dramas ensued, to be equaled only by a fender bender in Rome, with all the parties to the accident explaining to the policeman the rightness of their case, all at the same time. There came a time when Theo had actually won the argument, and the police- man was in the process of finding the chauffeur at fault, when Theo, bless him, just had to add the "coup de grace" and declared "if this idiot had been parked ten centimeters closer to the curb, I would have missed him altogether." You know who was ultimately convicted...

Theo could never leave well enough alone.

There came a time, as World War II approached, when Theo and Anna temporarily gave up their dreams of theatre and art, and they returned to the land of her birth, Luxembourg, and founded a small business.

Theo's experiences in that regard struck a special chord with me. In Arkansas, where I was raised, there was an old saying "don't get above your raisin".

Let me explain.

In certain societies, if your father was a coal miner, or a farmer, or a logger, you were expected to follow the same path. A fellow who went off to the city and acquired "city ways" was perceived as a

"Winter"
oil on paper
5.5" x 8.5"

traitor, of sorts. A shameful ingrate for rising above what his parents had achieved, or pretending to. If your father spoke the local dialect, you were "puttin' on airs" if you dared utter a sentence in grammatically correct English. This excuse for laziness and non-performance holds true to this day in some communities.

This then was the atmosphere in which Theo and Anna found themselves in those pre-war years. But in spite of it, until the war came, they prospered.

When war did come, Theo's interest in the arts, and disinterest in politics, required him to do what he could to prevent the looting of local art treasures.

The politics of it all would take a whole book to sort out, but suffice it to say, that while the grand ducal family were living out the war in England, comfortably enough, Theo and others like him were "minding the store". With tricks, diplomacy, and outright subterfuge and chicanery, those folks kept most, if not all of the country's art treasures, intact through two occupations by the Germans and two liberations by the Americans.

Curiously, the royals came out regarded as heroes for making broadcasts of encouragement to the folks in Luxembourgish (a language which had to be learned for the purpose, since the royal family spoke only French). Those who stayed and fought quietly to preserve the nation's treasures were later regarded as conspirators. It was a convenient way, it is commonly believed, to excuse royal cowardice, and to direct American reparations payments into the treasury, in the event the prince consort might need funds for a card game. (He had once lost the national forest in Monte Carlo, so the story goes, but the people bought it back.)

It is this curious and complex life that you will see in Theo's paintings. The rebel, the patriot, the democrat, the cynic, the man next door.

"Blue Peach Bowl"
oil on canvas board
20" x 30"
Courtesy Diane Fletcher

When Theo came to Elam with Catherine and me in 1977, he could not really grasp the fact that one family, just one family, could possibly own so much land. It was just about fifty acres but Theo was in awe of it. Shortly after we moved onto the land, into an old farmhouse, the origins of it dating back more than two hundred years, I took him for a walk around the borders of the property. From time to time he would stop. "Zhim, we go too far, this is anodder's land?"

"No", I would explain, "this is our land, we bought it ". And we would continue walking. But Theo was not easy in his mind about it.

Finally, when I showed him a plat map of the farm, and pointed out certain landmarks, and stones, and old iron rod markers, he became aware of the extent of fifty or so acres, and declared that "ve are barons".

In Theo's experience, only the very rich owned such vast expanses of land.

"Sunrise in Elam"   oil on canvas   34" x 24"

I never bothered to explain to him that ours was a mere flyspeck when compared to large American landowners. He was impressed. And once you have impressed such a man, you care little to "un-impress" him. If Theo wanted to regard himself as "the baron of Elam" that was fine with me. Monet had his Giverny...Theo had his Elam, and the world is richer for both of them. The world simply doesn't know enough about one of them.

Elam generated paintings. Theo never tired of depicting scenes of Elam in summer, winter, and in dreams. One of the finest, "The Elam Dream Scene" is one of those that best depicts his ability to rearrange things the way God would have arranged them if He had been fully aware of what He had to work with. Theo created flowers, and weather, and nature, as he felt it could be, and possibly, should be.

He "re-invented" dogwood and camellias, and irises, and roses, and gave them spirits and souls and sadness and joy, and did it all with an intensity that is hard to describe.

"I haf mak a beauty ting", was an announcement of the completion of something that was truly from Theo's soul.

Theo never doubted his work. And neither do I. You must decide for yourself. I leave it at that. And so would he.

Epilogue

When Theo Wildanger's health began to fail, about one year before he died, he moved from his beloved "barony" at Elam into the Weyanoke Inn, a retirement home in nearby Farmville, Virginia.

He quickly became a "celebrity guest", especially among the ladies, who were charmed with his old world manners.

There, he turned his room into a studio, painting dozens of new works, many of which found their way onto the walls of some of Farmville's leading families. His gifts to his fellow residents, and the Weyanoke Inn, would constitute a major collection in their own right.

Since his death, two shows have extended Theo's circle of admirers and collectors, and his works are currently on display in several cities in the United States and Europe. Several additional shows are in the planning stages.

The Wildanger Collection Ltd. was organized by his family and friends to provide a vehicle for their belief that Theo's work should reach as broad an audience as possible. This book is but a beginning.